Theme 4 · S0-ATZ-890

HOUGHTON MIFFLIN
Reading
A Legacy of Literacy

Problem
Solvers

HOUGHTON MIFFLIN · BOSTON · MORRIS PLAINS, NJ

California · Colorado · Georgia · Illinois · New Jersey · Texas

Design, Art Management and Page Production: Kirchoff/Wohlberg, Inc.

ILLUSTRATION CREDITS
4-21 Eric Velasquez. **22-39** Lori Lohstoeter. **40-57** Colin Bootman.
58-75 Raul Colon.

PHOTOGRAPHY CREDITS
22 PhotoDisc. **39** PhotoDisc. **40** David Robinson/Corbis. **57** David
Robinson/Corbis.

Printed in U.S.A.

ISBN: 0-618-04401-9

11 12 13 14 - VH - 06 05 04 03

Problem Solvers

Contents

The Best Fish Ever

The Drama Club is having tryouts for

The Fisherman and His Four Wishes

November 17   3:30 PM

by Julio Varela
illustrated by Eric Velasquez

Strategy Focus

Manny just knows he will get the lead in the school play. As you read, use clues from the story to **predict** what will happen.

Too Excited to Eat

It was only 7:30 A.M., but Manny was almost out the door. Ever since he started fourth grade three months ago, he had been waiting for this day to come.

"Mom, don't forget," Manny called on his way out. "Today after school I'll be with the Drama Club. We're having tryouts for the play."

"I know, I know," Manny's mom said. "You've been talking about it for the last three months. You're not having breakfast?"

"I'm too excited to eat," said Manny. "See you later!"

"Good luck!" Manny's mom said as she closed the door.

As he waited for the elevator, all Manny could think about was the tryouts.

This year Mr. Greene, the drama teacher, turned the story "The Fisherman and His Four Wishes" into a play. The play had only three main characters — the fisherman, his wife, and the magic fish who could grant wishes.

Mr. Greene wrote a happy ending for the play. When the fisherman loses everything because of his foolish wishes, the fish feels sorry for him and grants him a *fourth* wish. Luckily, the fisherman has finally learned his lesson and wishes for something of real value.

It was going to be a great play. More than anything, Manny wanted to play the part of the fisherman.

Who will Be the Fisherman?

"Mr. Greene says I would make a good fisherman," Manny said to his best friend, Nick.

Nick looked up from his tuna sandwich. He took a sip of milk before talking to his friend. "Are you forgetting something? You still have to try out. I mean, everyone wants to be the fisherman. Marcus, Guillermo, Richie, Ahmad, even Elena," Nick said.

"I know, but come on, you know I'm the best," Manny said. "I already know all the lines."

"I still think you should wait until you try out. What if you don't get it?" Nick asked.

"Yeah, right," Manny said, as if there were no chance of disappointment.

Nick shrugged his shoulders and went back to his sandwich.

The Drama Club
is having tryouts for

**The Fisherman and
His Four Wishes**

November 17   3:30 PM

The Tryouts

After school, Manny sat with the other Drama Club members and listened to Mr. Greene's instructions. "Okay, everyone, thanks for coming. When I call your name, please join me in the other room. You'll read your lines to me in there."

"Too bad," Manny thought. "Everyone but Mr. Greene will miss my tryout performance."

First Mr. Greene called Elena, then Marcus, Richie, Guillermo, and Ahmad. Finally he called, "Manny Rodríguez."

Manny bolted from his seat, looked around to see how many others were waiting, and shouted, "Yes, sir, I'm ready!"

Mr. Greene gave Manny a script. Then he said, "Okay, Manny, in this scene you will read the part of the fisherman, and I will read the part of the fish. This is when the fisherman makes the wish to live in a castle. Ready? Let's go."

Manny began to read his lines. He knew every one of them by heart. This was too easy.

The Telephone Call

That night Manny sat at the kitchen table, trying to do his math homework. But all he could think about was Mr. Greene announcing, "Manny Rodríguez will be the fisherman."

Suddenly, the phone rang, jolting Manny from his daydream. It was Mr. Greene. "Manny, you did a good job today, and I've decided to give you the part of . . ."

This is it, Manny thought. Say it's the fisherman.

". . . the fish."

"The *what*?" Manny yelped. "But Mr. Greene, I *really* want to be the fisherman. I know all the lines."

"So do a lot of the other kids," said Mr. Greene. "I gave that part to Ahmad. I think he'll make a great fisherman. *You* are going to make a great fish. Besides, the fish has the funniest lines in the play."

Mr. Greene took a deep breath and went on. "Manny, you are lucky. Lots of kids won't even be in the play. If you'd rather not play the fish, I'm sure I can find someone who will."

Manny didn't know what to say, and for a moment he was quiet. He then said good-bye to Mr. Greene.

As he got ready for bed, Manny told his mom what had happened. "It's just not fair," Manny said.

"Manny," said his mom, "just think about what Mr. Greene said. You want to be in the play. You're lucky to have been chosen."

"Yeah, I'll think about it," Manny grumbled.
"Good night."

The Play

Six weeks had passed, and the first performance of "The Fisherman and His Four Wishes" had finally arrived. It seemed as if the whole school was there. As the curtain rose and the play began, Mr. Greene looked proudly at his actors. He was right — Ahmad was a great fisherman. Everyone in the audience thought so the moment he walked on the stage.

But on that afternoon, the audience's favorite was the fish. Manny flopped around the stage and said his funny fish lines. He did just what he told himself over the past six weeks. "If I have to be a fish, then I'll be the best fish ever!"

When the play ended, Manny heard nothing
but cheers.

Mr. Greene told everyone that the play was a
success because of their efforts. "I hope you'll all
try out for the play next year."

"I know I will," Manny said. "But can I play
a person next time?"

Responding

Think About the Selection

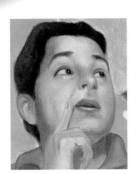

1 What play will the Drama Club present?

2 How does Manny feel about his tryout?

3 What prediction does Mr. Greene make that turns out to be right?

Predicting Outcomes

Copy this web on a piece of paper. Read the prediction. Then write details from the story to support it.

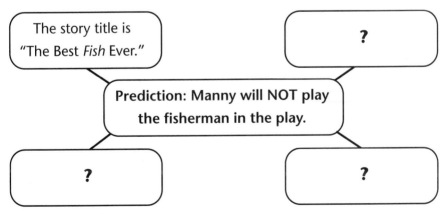

The story title is "The Best *Fish* Ever."

?

Prediction: Manny will NOT play the fisherman in the play.

?

?

Cora
at
Camp Blue Waters

by Philemon Sturges

illustrated by
Lori Lohstoeter

Strategy Focus

Cora is going to summer camp, even though she doesn't want to! As you read, **evaluate** what Cora does to solve her problems.

Cora was an indoor girl, a homebody. Her favorite hobby was drawing. She mostly drew the ideas in her head. "I like to use my imagination," she said.

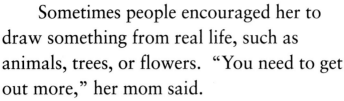

Sometimes people encouraged her to draw something from real life, such as animals, trees, or flowers. "You need to get out more," her mom said.

"It's more interesting in here," she told her mom, pointing to her own head.

In fact, Cora hardly noticed what was around her at all, except for what she called "the yucky things" — bugs and snakes.

So Cora was less than excited when her dad said that she'd be going to Camp Blue Waters that summer.

"Why me?" wailed Cora.

"Mom and I think you'd like the great outdoors if you'd give it a chance," said Cora's dad. "Besides, it's only for two weeks. Your pens and paper will be here when you get back."

"Your cousin Teri's going too! She went to Camp Blue Waters last summer, and she loved it," said Cora's mom. "You told me you never get to spend enough time with Teri. Here's your chance."

Cora couldn't fall asleep that night. She kept thinking about what was waiting for her at Camp Blue Waters. (Cora's imagination helped her draw, but it didn't help her sleep.) Ugh, thought Cora. I'm going to spend the next two weeks sweating and itching in the hot sun.

Even the thought of being with Teri didn't help.

Cora didn't sleep well during her first night at Camp Blue Waters, either. Things weren't quite as bad as she thought they'd be, but there *were* flies buzzing near the screen, and there *was* a spider in the shower. Moths flew around and around the light outside her cabin door. Owls hooted in the trees. Even Teri made noises in her sleep. And Cora just knew there was a bear nearby.

The next morning, it rained. Still, Cora and Teri's camp leader, Anne, took everyone outside for a tour of the camp.

They passed smooth playing fields and softly rolling hills. They saw a still, dark lake with a pale, sandy beach. Then they walked through the deep, green woods.

But all Cora saw was poison ivy, thorns, and sticks that looked like snakes. When she jumped away from one especially snaky stick, she slipped on some wet grass and fell into a muddy puddle.

Cora was nearly in tears when Anne and Teri pulled her up.

Anne said, "Let's get out of the rain for a little while." She led the girls to a large building. Inside was a huge room with a stage at one end and folding chairs at the other.

"This is where we put on plays and concerts," she said. Then she led them to another room.

Anne opened the door and said, "And this is the arts and crafts room." It was filled with big tables and easels. There were boxes of pencils, paints, and scissors. And there were shelves of paper, all kinds of paper.

"And this is the arts and crafts teacher, Bill," said Anne. Bill gave the girls a friendly wink.

Neat, thought Cora. Now if I could just stay in this room for two weeks. . . .

Cora *did* go to the arts and crafts room every day. But she didn't stay there. Bill often told everyone to pack up their paper and pencils and paints and go outside.

"But why?" Cora asked, the first time they went out. "I have plenty of ideas in my own head. I don't need to look at things outside."

But Bill told her, "An artist always uses what's inside, even when she draws outside. Just give it a try! I'll be there to help."

Bill showed Cora how to choose colors that matched nature. He taught her to see shapes and patterns in the leaves, and how to make living things look round on flat paper. He taught her to draw flowers, bugs, fish, and a rabbit she saw on the lawn.

When Cora showed Bill her drawing of two robins in a twisty old apple tree, he called her a "real wildlife artist."

Now when Cora drew outdoors, she wasn't bothered by poison ivy, or thorns, or bugs. She was too busy noticing the blue petals that matched the color of the sky. And when she saw sticks that looked like snakes, she wished they *were* snakes, so she could draw them.

After she got home, Cora kept drawing outside as much as she could. One snowy day, as she sat indoors drawing the beautiful ideas that lived in her head, she noticed that the outside had come in.

Responding

Think About the Selection

1. Who is Cora's cousin?
2. At the beginning of the story, what is Cora's problem with the outdoors?
3. How is Cora's problem solved?

Problem Solving

Copy the chart on a piece of paper. Read about camp leader Anne's problem. Write any solutions you read about in the story. Can you think of any others to write?

Anne's Problem	Solutions
It's a rainy day at the camp.	• Have the children dress in rain gear and take them out anyway. • ? • ?

39

Murals for Joy

by Veronica Freeman Ellis
illustrated by Colin Bootman

YOUTH CENTER

Strategy Focus

Joy doesn't think she'll have a good time in the city. As you read, stop once in a while to **summarize** what has happened.

Celia and her mother, Mrs. Delaney, lived in the city. Every summer Celia visited her cousin Joy. Joy lived near the seashore with her parents.

When Celia visited, the girls played on the beach and swam. Sometimes they went sailing with Joy's parents.

This summer was different. Joy was
spending four weeks with Celia in the city.

The girls sat outside Celia's apartment
building.

"Is sitting on the steps all you do?"
asked Joy.

"No," answered Celia, "but it's fun
watching people."

"I don't think it's fun," grumbled Joy. "If we were at my house, we'd be swimming, or we'd be sailing around the bay."

"City people do different things for fun," said Celia. "After four weeks, you may like what we do."

"Maybe I will," said Joy. "Or maybe I won't."

The next day the girls went to the Youth Center. "This is my cousin," Celia told the other children. "She'll be coming to the center with me this summer."

The group leader, Ms. Howard, invited Joy to join them in the day's activities.

Ms. Howard told the children they would be talking about important African-Americans. Later they would make posters of the people they liked and wanted to learn more about.

In the afternoon Ms. Howard helped the children make sweet potato pie. They ate the pie at snack time.

"Mmmmmm," said Joy. "This pie is dee-licious!"

That evening Mrs. Delaney asked, "Joy, did you have some fun?"

"Not much," mumbled Joy. "I'd have more fun at home."

"Why don't you take her back home, Mom?" asked Celia.

"Give her time," said Mrs. Delaney. "I know she'll like the city."

"Maybe I will," said Joy. "Or maybe I won't."

The next day, Ms. Howard talked about
Frederick Douglass, who fought slavery. She
also talked about the musicians Duke Ellington
and Wynton Marsalis and the writer Toni
Morrison. Joy thought their lives sounded
interesting and exciting. She asked many
questions when Ms. Howard finished.

That evening Joy said, "Aunt Nancy, will you please take us to the library?"

"Certainly," said Mrs. Delaney. "What books do you want?"

"Books on Toni Morrison," answered Joy. "And the musicians Duke Ellington and Wynton Marsalis. Ms. Howard told us about all of them today."

Celia and Mrs. Delaney looked at each other and smiled. They were happy something interested Joy.

"Tomorrow's Saturday, so I don't have to work," said Mrs. Delaney. "We'll spend the morning at the library."

"Sounds good, Mom, but can we go to the center first?" said Celia. "I left my good sweater there yesterday."

A crowd was outside the Youth Center on Saturday morning. Everyone was talking at the same time.

"What's going on?" asked Mrs. Delaney and the girls.

"Somebody wrote all over the center's walls," Ms. Howard answered.

"How awful!" exclaimed Joy. "What can we do about it?"

"We're having a meeting in the auditorium now," said Ms. Howard. "Please join us."

When Mrs. Delaney and the girls sat down, the center's director began to speak. "Of course, we'll paint the walls," she said.

"But what about later on?" asked Ms. Howard. "Those who wrote on the walls will do so again."

The director asked for ideas to stop the writing.

Joy waved her hand, but the director didn't see her.

Mrs. Delaney stood and said, "Joy wants to speak."

"Let's paint murals that show important African-Americans," said Joy. "Murals will make it hard to write on the walls."

Everyone liked Joy's idea and agreed to paint murals.

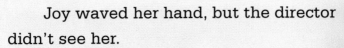

First, everyone helped to paint over the writing. Then neighborhood artists drew pictures of the important African-Americans everyone had agreed on.

Then everyone helped the artists to paint in the outlined pictures.

Joy worked with others on the mural of
Toni Morrison. Celia helped with the mural of
Wynton Marsalis. Then they worked together
on the mural of Martin Luther King, Jr. One
Saturday, Mrs. Delaney worked with them on
the mural of Duke Ellington.

"The murals are wonderful," said Mrs. Delaney when they were finished. "The center looks even better than it did before."

"Yes, it does," agreed Ms. Howard. "And I hope people will be too proud of these important African-Americans to write on their faces!"

"You're going home in two days, Joy," said Mrs. Delaney. "I know," said Joy. "Four weeks went by quickly."

"I'm sure you'll be back next summer," said Mrs. Delaney.

"Maybe she won't," said Celia.

Joy smiled and said, "Maybe I will."

Responding

Think About the Selection

1. Why does Celia like to sit on the apartment building steps?

2. Why do you think the director asks for ideas to stop the writing?

3. What clues in the story tell you that Joy's feelings about her summer in the city are changing?

Drawing Conclusions

Copy the chart on a piece of paper. Read the conclusion. Then complete the chart by writing two more clues that lead to the conclusion.

Clues	Conclusion
They have a meeting to figure out how to clean the walls.	The community is proud of the appearance of their Youth Center.
?	
?	

Ruthie's Perfect Poem

by Andrew Clements
illustrated by
Raul Colón

Ruthie is too shy to read her poems out loud. As you read, ask **questions** about how she will overcome her shyness.

Ruthie Carter loved to imagine. She looked at a mud puddle, and she saw an ocean. She looked at a bookcase, and she saw a skyscraper.

But when Ruthie looked at herself, she saw nothing — just a shy girl who scribbled poems in a secret notebook.

Ruthie didn't like it when people looked at her. She kept her hair down in front of her eyes. That way she had a place to hide.

Ruthie never raised her hand in class, even when she had the right answer. When the teacher asked her to read out loud, Ruthie pretended she had a sore throat.

When it was time to work in groups, Ruthie looked down at her shoes, hoping she wouldn't be picked for one. That way she could work all by herself.

One day Ruthie's teacher said, "Mary DeLaney is coming to visit our school."

Ruthie couldn't believe it. Mary DeLaney wrote wonderful poems and stories. She was Ruthie's favorite author!

Ruthie's teacher said, "Mary DeLaney wants me to send her some of your stories and poems. If you have something to share with her, put it in this box by tomorrow afternoon."

At home that night, Ruthie looked in her secret notebook. She chose a poem called "My Couch." It was one of her favorites. Ruthie used her best handwriting and made a copy of the poem.

The next day at school, Ruthie waited until she thought no one was watching. Then she put her poem into the box.

At the end of the day, the teacher mailed all the stories and poems to Mary DeLaney.

A week later, Ruthie's class got a letter from Mary DeLaney. The teacher read the letter. Then she said, "This is good news. When Mary DeLaney talks to you and your parents tomorrow night, she wants some of you to read your poems and stories to everyone."

Then the teacher read five names — and first on the list was Ruthie Carter!

Ruthie worried all day long. She thought, "What if I trip going up to the stage? What if my voice is too soft? What if everyone laughs at me?"

At home Ruthie told her mom and dad what
happened. Her mom said, "That's great! You are
such a wonderful writer!"

Ruthie said, "But everyone will be looking
at me!"

Then she ran to her room and slammed the
door.

Ruthie's dad came to her room. He said,
"These are some of my old report cards. Take a
look."

Ruthie read what the teachers said about her
dad. "David needs to speak up in class." "David
is a good reader, but he will not read out loud."

Ruthie's dad said, "Once I had to read a speech by President Lincoln. I told my mom I was too scared. And your grandma told me, 'David, just stop thinking about yourself all the time!' — so I did, and it worked!"

Ruthie said, "Well, maybe that worked for you, but nothing can help me."

The next night, a nervous Ruthie sat with her
mom and dad and grandma at the assembly.
When Mary DeLaney called her name, Ruthie felt
like a ball of tangled string.

Her grandma smiled and patted her hand.
She whispered, "Now Ruthie, don't think about
how you are feeling — instead, think how much
I'm going to love hearing you read."

Ruthie shook hands with Mary DeLaney and then started to read.

My Couch

Each Saturday at half past three,
My old gray couch says, "Come with me."
I stretch out flat, I close my eyes.
The couch lifts off the floor and flies!

Out we go, then over trees,
Beyond the hills, across the seas.
We fly through jungles green and deep.
I see the tigers crouch and creep.
We fly above the desert sands.
I wave at camel caravans.

It's wonderful to feel so free,
But something always puzzles me.
It matters not how far we roam,
By dinnertime, we're always home.

When Ruthie stopped reading, it was quiet
— but just for a second. Then everyone clapped,
and some people even stood up and cheered.

Mary DeLaney said, "You read that poem
perfectly!" Then she gave Ruthie a new book and
a gold ribbon.

Ruthie's mom said, "Your dad and I are so proud of you!" Her grandma gave Ruthie a big hug. Then she said, "I heard every single word, loud and clear."

Ruthie said, "That's because I read my poem just for you!"

Responding

Think About the Selection

1. Who is Ruthie's favorite author?
2. Why do you think Ruthie is so shy?
3. How do you think Ruthie feels at the end of the story?

Story Structure

Copy this map on a piece of paper and then complete it.

Title	*Ruthie's Perfect Poem*			
Setting	*Where*	?		
	When	?		
Characters	Ruthie	?	?	?
Beginning	Ruthie likes to daydream and write poems. But she is shy about sharing them with anyone.			
Middle	?			
End	?			